Grandparent's Memory Book
for Jewish Families

GRANDPARENT'S MEMORY BOOK
FOR
JEWISH FAMILIES

Created by
The Sisterhood
of
Congregation Beth El
Bethesda, Maryland

Editor
Marsha Rehns

Writers
Evelyn Bitterbaum
Patricia Danoff
N. Amanda Ford
Judith Cantor Goldman
Deborah Golub Leibowitz
Margery London
Holly Stein

Family Tree
Tamar Fishman

Acknowledgements

The editor and writers of *Grandparent's Memory Book for Jewish Families* wish to thank the members of the Sisterhood of Congregation Beth El of Montgomery County, Bethesda, Maryland, for their careful review, suggestions, criticisms, financial support, and encouragement.

In particular, we are grateful to Judith Baldinger, Rita Kahn, Linda Lipson, Doris Povich, Marta Wassertzug, and Ina Young for their comments on a work in progress, to Tamar Fishman and Hal Scheinberg for the Hebrew quotations, and to Joni Sussman of Kar-Ben and Michele Lieban Levine for help with publishing.

This
GRANDPARENT'S MEMORY BOOK
FOR JEWISH FAMILIES

was completed by

_____

beginning on

_____

and ending on

_____

because

_____
_____
_____
_____
_____
_____
_____

_____
Signature

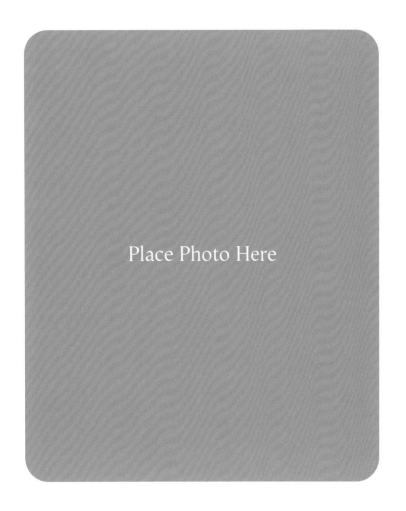

Place Photo Here

Table of Contents

INTRODUCTION

Dear Grandparent,

Welcome to the *Grandparent's Memory Book for Jewish Families!*

The first thing you'll notice about this book is that it asks you for many responses. You may not be able to complete them all. Some topics may not apply to you. Others you may choose to skip over. If you can't recall a piece of information, leave the item blank and come back to it later. You may find that having filled in other parts of the book first helps you remember.

Please don't try to fill out the entire book in one sitting. And don't feel you have to do the sections in order. You may want to dictate your responses to someone else to write down. Asking your child or grandchild to help you is a wonderful way to share your memories and create new ones.

I will bestow my blessing upon you and make your descendants as numerous as the stars of heaven and the sands on the seashore. (Genesis: 22:17)

כִּי־בָרֵךְ אֲבָרֶכְךָ וְהַרְבָּה אַרְבֶּה אֶת־זַרְעֲךָ כְּכוֹכְבֵי הַשָּׁמַיִם וְכַחוֹל אֲשֶׁר עַל־שְׂפַת הַיָּם

Although this book is directed to Jewish families, we know that families are blended in many ways. We hope everyone will find a way to adapt the book to his or her circumstances.

We hope you enjoy your journey from the past into the future.

With a child in the house, all corners are full.
(Yiddish saying)

IN THE BEGINNING
Birth to 12 Years

My full name is _____
_____

I was named for _____
_____
_____

My Hebrew name is _____
_____

In Hebrew I was named for _____
_____
_____

My nicknames were _____
_____

    because _____
_____
_____

The way I felt about my name was _____
_____
_____
_____

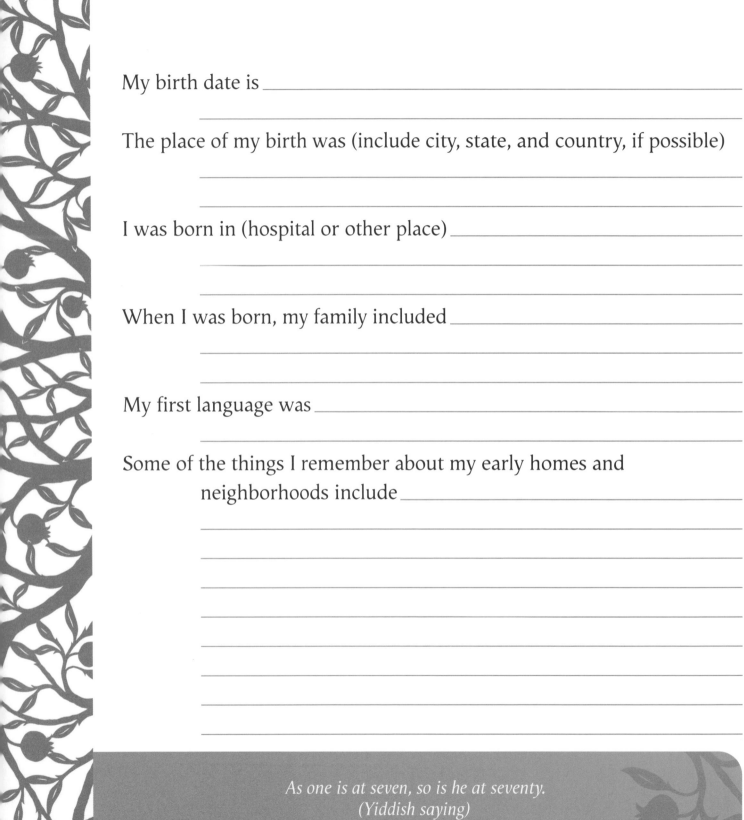

My birth date is _____
_____

The place of my birth was (include city, state, and country, if possible)
_____
_____

I was born in (hospital or other place) _____
_____
_____

When I was born, my family included _____
_____
_____

My first language was _____
_____

Some of the things I remember about my early homes and
     neighborhoods include _____
_____
_____
_____
_____
_____
_____
_____
_____

As one is at seven, so is he at seventy.
(Yiddish saying)

The schools I attended until I was 12 years old were _____

_____

_____

This is how I traveled to school _____

_____

_____

Some of my early friends were _____

_____

_____

_____

When I was by myself, some of my favorite toys or pastimes were

_____

_____

_____

_____

My favorite childhood book was _____

_____

I wanted to be _____ when I grew up.

Significant events in my life that I remember from these years are

_____

_____

_____

_____

_____

Significant events in the news that I remember from these years are

_____

_____

_____

_____

_____

Some special times/trips/celebrations I remember from my early life
     through age 12 are _____

_____

_____

_____

_____

_____

_____

Something else that I would like you to know about my
     early childhood is _____

_____

_____

_____

_____

_____

MY TEEN YEARS
Ages 13 to 18

During my teen years, ages 13-18, my family lived in these places

_____

_____

_____

The schools I attended during my teen years were _____

_____

_____

The last grade of high school I completed was _____ in the year

_____ when I was _____ years old.

My favorite subjects in school were _____

_____

_____

I liked them because _____

_____

_____

My least favorite subjects in school were _____

_____

_____

I disliked them because _____

_____

_____

13

My grades during these school years could be described as _____

_____

_____

My best friends during my teen years were _____

_____

_____

I am still in touch with _____

_____

_____

Some favorite things I did with my friends were _____

_____

_____

_____

As a teenager, some of the activities in which I participated (such as
academic, social, religious, sports, music, drama) were

_____

_____

_____

My favorite activity was _____

_____

I liked it because _____

_____

_____

_____

Household chores for which I was responsible included _____

_____

_____

_____

_____

The most difficult thing about being a teenager was _____

_____

_____

_____

_____

I would describe my relationship with my parents as _____

_____

_____

_____

_____

I would describe my relationship with my siblings as _____

_____

_____

_____

Significant events in my life that I remember from these years are

_____

_____

_____

_____

Ask advice from everyone, but act with your own mind.
(Yiddish saying)

Significant events in the news that I remember from these years are

_____

_____

_____

_____

_____

Something else about my teen years that I would like you
to know is _____

_____

_____

_____

_____

_____

_____

_____

_____

_____

_____

_____

_____

MY ADULT YEARS

Immediately after high school, I _____
_____
_____
_____

Job training I received included _____
_____
_____
_____

COLLEGE

I went to college at _____
        from _____ to _____ .

My major in college was _____
_____

The degree I received was _____
_____

Organizations or activities I participated in at college were
_____
_____
_____

Wisdom comes with the years.
(Yiddish saying)

While at college I lived in _____

_____

_____

Some special memories about my college years include _____

_____

_____

_____

_____

_____

The most important thing I learned from my college experience was

_____

_____

Additional degrees I received were _____

_____

MILITARY SERVICE

My service in the military included the years _____ to _____

The branch of the military in which I served was_____

My highest rank was _____

Some of my tours of duty included _____

_____

What I remember most about my military service is _____

_____

EMPLOYMENT

My first full-time job was _____

_____

_____

The different positions in which I worked over the years included

_____

_____

_____

My favorite job was _____

because _____

_____

RETIREMENT

I retired from _____ in _____

Since retiring, I spend my time _____

_____

_____

_____

Something I'd still like to do is _____

_____

_____

MARRIAGE/DIVORCE

I met your grandfather/grandmother (name) _____

        in (date) _____ at _____

The qualities that attracted me to him/her were _____

_____

_____

_____

_____

My favorite memories of our courtship are _____

_____

_____

_____

_____

Our wedding date was _____

We were married in (place) _____

        by _____

At our wedding, I wore _____

_____

_____

_____

Honor your father and mother, so your days may be long. (Exodus: 20:12)

כַּבֵּד אֶת־אָבִיךָ וְאֶת־אִמֶּךָ לְמַעַן יַאֲרִכוּן יָמֶיךָ

Among our guests were _____

_____

_____

_____

_____

This is how we celebrated after our wedding ceremony _____

_____

_____

_____

_____

For our honeymoon, we _____

_____

_____

_____

_____

Married life for me was/is _____

_____

_____

_____

_____

My marriage ended because _____

_____

_____

_____

_____

I was married more than once. Here's some information about that

_____

_____

_____

_____

Lessons I learned about marriage that I want you to know are

_____

_____

_____

_____

_____

_____

_____

_____

_____

_____

_____

_____

_____

PLACES I HAVE LIVED

As an adult, I lived in _____ different places.

First, I lived in _____

I moved there because _____

_____

Here are other places I lived and why I moved there: _____

_____

_____

MY CHILDREN

I have had _____ children. They are:

Name _____ Hebrew Name _____

We named this child after _____

_____

Date of birth _____ Place of birth _____

A wonderful memory I have of this child is _____

_____

_____

_____

_____

Name _____ Hebrew Name _____

We named this child after _____

_____

Date of birth _____ Place of birth _____

A wonderful memory I have of this child is _____

_____

_____

_____

_____

Name _____ Hebrew Name _____

We named this child after _____

_____

Date of birth _____ Place of birth _____

A wonderful memory I have of this child is _____

_____

_____

_____

_____

Name _____ Hebrew Name _____

We named this child after _____

_____

Date of birth _____ Place of birth _____

A wonderful memory I have of this child is _____

_____

_____

_____

_____

Name _____ Hebrew Name _____

We named this child after _____

_____

Date of birth _____ Place of birth _____

A wonderful memory I have of this child is _____

_____

_____

_____

_____

HOUSEHOLD ARRANGEMENTS

After our children were born, the household responsibilities were handled this way _____

_____

_____

The chief cook in our family was _____

_____

Some of our favorite foods were _____

_____

_____

In the evening after dinner, we often would _____

_____

_____

We usually went to bed at (time) _____
On weekends, we often would _____

_____

_____

_____

_____

_____

_____

INTERESTS AND HOBBIES

In my spare time I like to _____

_____

_____

_____

I have a collection of _____

_____

_____

_____

Over the years I have volunteered as _____

_____

_____

_____

REFLECTIONS

As I reflect on my adult life, I _____

_____

_____

_____

_____

_____

If I could live my life over again, I would _____

_____

_____

_____

During times of personal difficulty, I turn to _____

_____

_____

_____

_____

_____

_____

Other things I would like you to know about my life as an adult are _____

_____

_____

_____

_____

_____

_____

_____

_____

_____

GENERATIONS
Di Ganzeh Mishpocheh

ABOUT MY PARENTS

My father's name was _____

His Hebrew name was _____

My father's birthdate was _____

He was born in (city, state, country) _____
_____

My father's ancestors emigrated from _____
_____
_____

and settled in (include city, state, dates, etc.) _____
_____
_____
_____

Some of the jobs my father held included _____
_____
_____

Most of the time when I was growing up, he worked as a _____
_____

Whoever teaches their children, teaches not only their children but also their children's children and so on to the end of generations. (Talmud Kiddushin: 30a)

שֶׁכָּל הַמְלַמֵּד אֶת בְּנוֹ תּוֹרָה מַעֲלֶה עָלָיו הַכָּתוּב כְּאִילוּ לִמְּדוֹ לוֹ וְלִבְנוֹ
וּלְבֶן בְּנוֹ עַד סוֹף כָּל הַדּוֹרוֹת

My father died on _____ at the age of _____

The Hebrew date of his death (his *Yahrzeit*) is _____

The cause of his death, as far as I know, was _____

The name and location of the cemetery where he is buried are

_____

_____

A few of the special memories I have of my father are _____

_____

_____

_____

_____

_____

_____

_____

_____

My mother's maiden name was _____

Her Hebrew name was _____

My mother's birthdate was _____

She was born in (city, state, country) _____

_____

My mother's ancestors emigrated from _____

_____

_____

and settled in (include city, state, dates, etc.) _____

_____

_____

Some of the jobs my mother held included _____

_____

_____

Most of the time when I was growing up, she worked as a _____

_____

_____

My mother died on _____ at the age of _____

The Hebrew date of her death (her *Yahrzeit*) is _____

The cause of her death, as far as I know, was _____

The name and location of the cemetery where she is buried are

_____

_____

A few of the special memories I have of my mother are _____

_____

_____

_____

_____

_____

_____

_____

ABOUT MY SIBLINGS

I have had _____ brothers and _____ sisters. In the birth order, I was _____
My siblings' names (in order of their birth) are:

Name	Year Born	Year Died	Cause of Death

A few of the special memories I have of my siblings are _____

_____

_____

_____

_____

_____

_____

_____

_____

_____

_____

OTHER FAMILY MEMORIES

When I was born, our household included _____

_____

_____

_____

Special people in my life (extended family, friends, teachers, neighbors,
    household help, clergy, or others) were _____

_____

_____

_____

_____

Some of my family members including _____

_____

spoke a language other than English. The language was

_____

My ability to speak this language is _____
I would describe my family's economic status when I was growing up
    as _____

_____

_____

Family pets that I remember are _____

_____

_____

Some favorite family sayings, stories, or anecdotes that I remember are

_____

_____

_____

_____

_____

_____

_____

_____

_____

Heirlooms I have inherited, and to whom they belonged, are

_____

_____

_____

_____

_____

_____

Other special possessions I have are _____

_____

_____

_____

_____

_____

Remember the days of old; consider the generations long past. (Deuteronomy 32:7)

זְכֹר יְמוֹת עוֹלָם בִּינוּ שְׁנוֹת דֹּר וָדֹר

FAMILY MEDICAL HISTORY

Medical conditions that have occurred in our family include

_____

_____

_____

I am allergic to _____

_____

_____

My blood type is _____
My medical history has included _____

_____

_____

_____

Something else about my family that I would like you to
know is _____

_____

_____

_____

_____

_____

_____

Grandchild

Child ___ Grandchild

Grandchild

Grandchild

Child

Grandchild

Grandchild

Grandchild

Child

Child

Our
Family Tree

Grandparent's Father

Paternal Grandmother

Paternal Grandfather

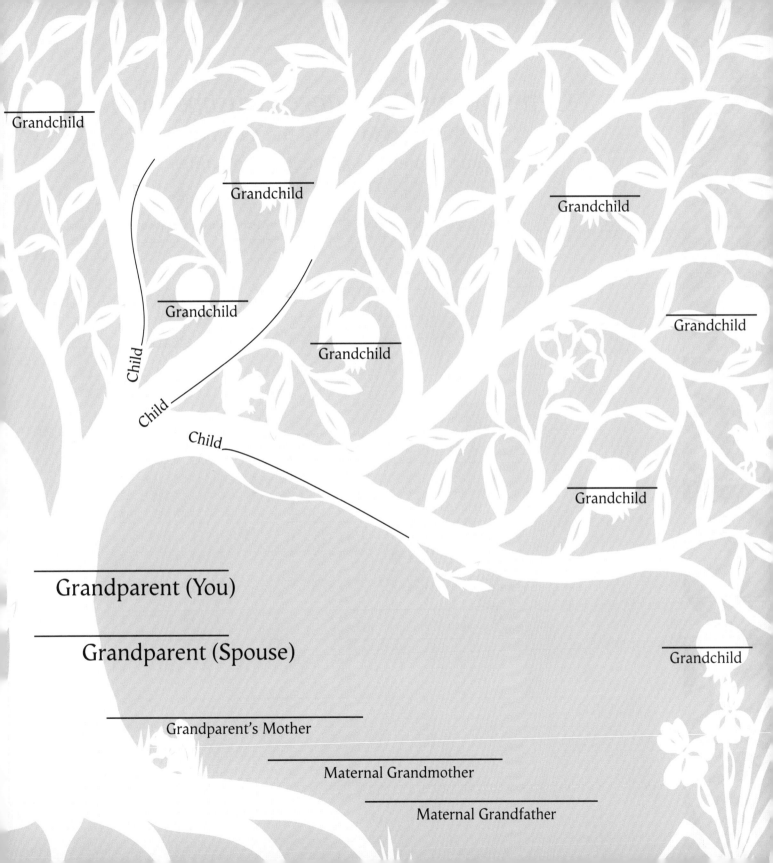

Grandchild

Grandchild

Grandchild

Grandchild

Grandchild

Child

Grandchild

Child

Grandchild

Child

Grandchild

Grandparent (You)

Grandparent (Spouse)

Grandchild

Grandparent's Mother

Maternal Grandmother

Maternal Grandfather

Generations (*Di Ganzeh Mishpocheh*)

Use this chart to record the members
of your immediate and extended family.

Name	Hebrew Name	Relationship to You	Date of Birth	Date of Death (*Yahrzeit*)

ON BEING A GRANDPARENT

My grandchildren call me _____

_____

    because _____

_____

_____

Special names I have for my grandchildren are _____

_____

_____

_____

_____

_____

I called my grandparents _____

_____

    because _____

_____

When I learned about the arrival of my first grandchild, I felt

_____

_____

_____

_____

_____

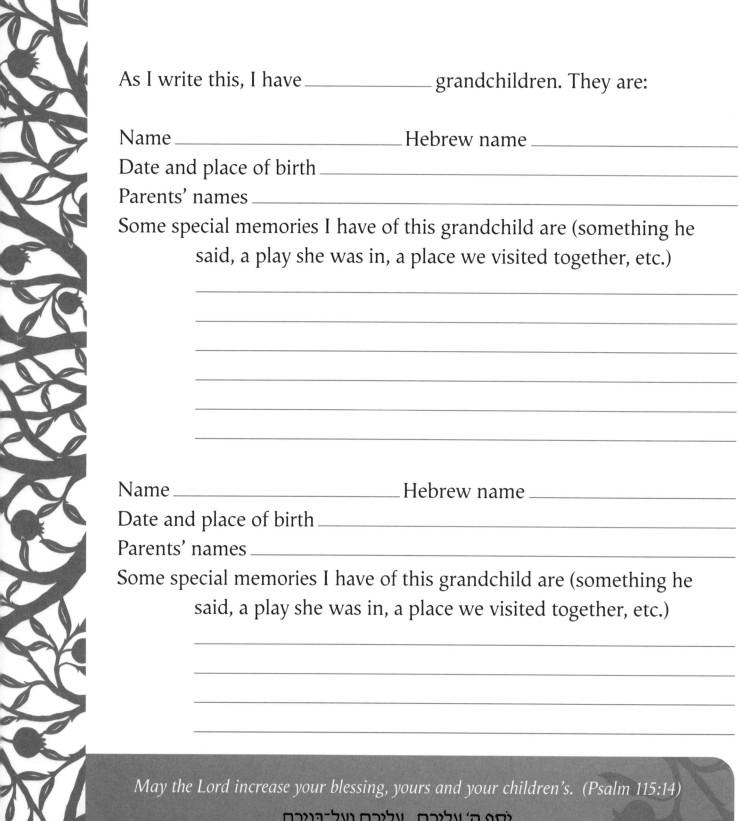

As I write this, I have _____ grandchildren. They are:

Name _____ Hebrew name _____
Date and place of birth _____
Parents' names _____
Some special memories I have of this grandchild are (something he
said, a play she was in, a place we visited together, etc.)

_____

_____

_____

_____

_____

_____

Name _____ Hebrew name _____
Date and place of birth _____
Parents' names _____
Some special memories I have of this grandchild are (something he
said, a play she was in, a place we visited together, etc.)

_____

_____

_____

_____

May the Lord increase your blessing, yours and your children's. (Psalm 115:14)

יֹסֵף ה' עֲלֵיכֶם, עֲלֵיכֶם וְעַל־בְּנֵיכֶם

_____

_____

_____

Name _____ Hebrew name _____

Date and place of birth _____

Parents' names _____

Some special memories I have of this grandchild are (something he
     said, a play she was in, a place we visited together, etc.)

_____

_____

_____

_____

_____

_____

Name _____ Hebrew name _____

Date and place of birth _____

Parents' names _____

Some special memories I have of this grandchild are (something he
     said, a play she was in, a place we visited together, etc.)

_____

_____

_____

_____

_____

_____

_____

_____

Name _____ Hebrew name _____

Date and place of birth _____

Parents' names _____

Some special memories I have of this grandchild are (something he
said, a play she was in, a place we visited together, etc.)

_____

_____

_____

_____

_____

_____

_____

Name _____ Hebrew name _____

Date and place of birth _____

Parents' names _____

Some special memories I have of this grandchild are (something he said, a play she was in, a place we visited together, etc.)

_____

_____

_____

_____

_____

_____

_____

Name _____ Hebrew name _____

Date and place of birth _____

Parents' names _____

Some special memories I have of this grandchild are (something he
said, a play she was in, a place we visited together, etc.)

_____

_____

_____

_____

_____

_____

_____

Name _____ Hebrew name _____

Date and place of birth _____

Parents' names _____

Some special memories I have of this grandchild are (something he
    said, a play she was in, a place we visited together, etc.)

_____

_____

_____

_____

_____

_____

_____

The Jewish holidays and life cycle events I enjoy celebrating with my
    grandchildren are _____

_____

_____

_____

_____

Some non-Jewish holidays and events I celebrate with my
    grandchildren are _____

_____

_____

_____

Some of the things I enjoy doing with my grandchildren (trips, visits, activities, events) are _____

_____

_____

_____

_____

Filling out this section on being a grandparent led me to these additional thoughts _____

_____

_____

_____

_____

_____

_____

_____

_____

_____

_____

_____

_____

_____

_____

HOLIDAYS AND TRADITIONS

RELIGIOUS TRADITIONS

I was raised in a (fill in religion) _____ home.

My family was (fill in level of observance) _____ observant.

When I was growing up, the religious holidays we celebrated at home were (for Jewish holidays, refer to list at end of this section)

_____

_____

_____

_____

_____

My favorite home holiday celebration was _____ because

_____

When I was growing up, the synagogue (church) I belonged to was

_____

The religious holidays we celebrated at our synagogue (church) were

_____

_____

_____

My favorite synagogue (church) holiday was _____

because _____

_____

When my children were growing up, the religious holidays our family
celebrated were _____

_____

_____

_____

_____

Now, my favorite religious holiday is _____

because _____

_____

_____

_____

My favorite traditions are _____

_____

_____

_____

My favorite holiday foods are _____

_____

_____

_____

Special holiday guests have included _____

_____

_____

_____

In the first month, on the fourteenth day,
in the evening you shall eat matzah. (Exodus 12:18)

בָּרִאשֹׁן בְּאַרְבָּעָה עָשָׂר יוֹם לַחֹדֶשׁ בָּעֶרֶב תֹּאכְלוּ מַצֹּת

RELIGIOUS EDUCATION

My religious education included _____

_____

_____

_____

_____

_____

What I remember most about my religious education is

_____

_____

_____

_____

_____

I became a Bar/Bat Mitzvah on _____ at _____

My Torah portion was _____

We celebrated by _____

_____

_____

_____

_____

_____

I was confirmed on _____ at _____

Other significant religious events in my life were

_____

_____

_____

_____

_____

_____

_____

_____

Other religious ceremonies in which I have participated included

_____

_____

_____

_____

_____

_____

_____

_____

Jewish holidays: Shabbat, Rosh Hashanah, Yom Kippur, Sukkot, Simchat Torah, Hanukkah, Purim, Pesach, Shavuot

SECULAR CELEBRATIONS

Secular holidays I have enjoyed celebrating are _____

_____

_____

_____

_____

_____

_____

_____

In particular, I celebrate _____ this way

_____

_____

_____

_____

_____

_____

My most memorable birthday was _____

_____

_____

_____

_____

_____

ON BEING JEWISH
MY JUDAISM

Growing up Jewish meant that _____

_____

_____

_____

Being Jewish influenced my life in these ways _____

_____

_____

_____

Today the role that Judaism plays in my life is _____

_____

_____

_____

My concept of God is _____

_____

_____

_____

My involvement with the Jewish community has included _____

_____

_____

_____

_____

Throughout the ages, Jews have been subjected to anti-Semitism. My experience with discrimination has been _____

_____

_____

_____

_____

WORLD WAR II AND THE HOLOCAUST

During World War II, I was _____

_____

_____

_____

The Holocaust affected my family in these ways _____

_____

_____

_____

_____

Family members lost in the Holocaust include _____

_____

_____

_____

_____

ERETZ YISRAEL

About the creation of the State of Israel in 1948, I remember _____

_____

_____

_____

The significance of the State of Israel to me is _____

_____

_____

_____

_____

_____

My first trip to Israel was _____

_____

_____

_____

_____

_____

To learn the whole Talmud is a great accomplishment;
to learn one good virtue is even greater.
(Yiddish saying)

Other trips to Israel or to places of Jewish significance include

_____

_____

_____

Filling out this section on being Jewish has led me to these additional thoughts _____

_____

_____

_____

_____

_____

_____

_____

_____

_____

_____

_____

_____

_____

INTERESTING TIDBITS
My *Mishegoss*

My favorite season is _____ because _____

My favorite time of day is _____ because _____

My favorite book is _____

because _____

My favorite flower is _____

My favorite comfort foods are _____

My favorite color is _____

My favorite smell is _____

When I was a child, I was afraid of _____

Now I am afraid of _____

I have a superstition about _____

I ran away from _____ when _____

_____

My preference in music is _____

My favorite singer is _____

My favorite musician/band is _____

My favorite TV/radio show when I was growing up was _____

_____

The kinds of movies I like best are _____

My favorite sports team is _____

Every person has his own mishegoss (idiosyncrasies).
(Yiddish saying)

The political party/position I support is _____

My worst habit is _____

My best habit is _____

The habit I would like to start is _____

The habit that other people have that drives me up a wall is _____
_____

My pet peeve is _____

My best quality is _____

My worst quality is _____

Other people would describe me as _____
_____

I would describe my character as _____

The one thing I would like to change about the way I look is _____
_____
_____

My hero is/was _____

The most comfortable room in my house is/was _____
because _____

Special things I like to do are _____

My idea of a great vacation is _____

The person I talk to every day or almost every day is _____
_____

For exercise, I like to _____

He who is aware of his folly is wise.
(Yiddish saying)

When I read a newspaper, the first section I turn to is _____
_____

I envy _____
I regret _____
I have never had enough time for _____
The one thing I haven't done in my life that I would like to do is
_____
_____

A favorite time of my life was _____

_____
_____
_____
_____
_____
_____
_____
_____
_____
_____
_____
_____
_____
_____

FIRSTS AND SUPERLATIVES

My earliest memory is from when I was (age) _____
      I remember _____
_____
_____

My first trip with my parents was when I was (age) _____
      We went to _____
_____
_____

My first trip without my parents was when I was (age) _____
      I went to _____
_____
_____

My first trip to another country was when I was (age) _____
      I went to _____
_____
_____

I took my first airplane ride was when I was (age) _____
      I went to _____
_____
_____

My favorite vacation was _____
_____

My first kiss was with _____ when I was (age) _____

    I thought it was _____

    _____

My first paying job was _____ when I was (age) _____

    I earned _____

    I thought the job was _____

    _____

The best meal I ever ate was _____

    _____

    It was memorable because _____

    _____

    _____

My best friend's name was/is _____

The best decade of my life was _____

The worst decade of my life was _____

The happiest day of my life was when _____

_____

_____

_____

The luckiest day of my life was when _____

_____

_____

_____

Things can't be bad all the time, nor good all the time.
(Yiddish saying)

The worst day of my life was when _____

_____

_____

_____

The hardest thing I ever had to do was _____

_____

    I thought the outcome was _____

_____

_____

The most embarrassing thing I ever did was when I was (age) _____

    Here's what happened _____

_____

_____

The funniest thing that ever happened to me was _____

_____

_____

_____

My proudest accomplishment is _____

_____

_____

    because _____

_____

_____

The worst disaster I have lived through was _____

_____

_____

My biggest mistake was _____

_____

_____

The best decision I ever made was _____

_____

_____

The most influential person in my life was _____

_____

_____

The most extravagant thing I ever did was _____

_____

_____

_____

Man is like a breath, his days are like a passing shadow...So teach us to treasure our days; then we shall acquire a heart of wisdom. (Psalms 144:4, 90:12)

אָדָם לַהֶבֶל דָּמָה יָמָיו כְּצֵל עוֹבֵר... לִמְנוֹת יָמֵינוּ כֵּן הוֹדַע וְנָבִא לְבַב חָכְמָה

HOW TIMES HAVE CHANGED

The world is different today than when I was younger. I think the most significant invention created since I was born is _____

_____

    because _____

_____

Household conveniences are different today too. The thing I remember being the hardest to do around the house that is easier today is

_____

_____

To write a school report, I _____

_____

_____

What was different about clothing when I was a child was _____

_____

_____

We got our first television when I was _____ years old. My favorite shows were _____

_____

_____

What I remember most about that TV is _____

_____

_____

Making a telephone call was different. The phone was (describe how the phone looked and other things you remember about the phone)

_____

_____

_____

To place a long distance call, you had to _____

_____

_____

The first car I owned was _____

The thing I remember most about that car is _____

_____

_____

Things that we had then that we don't have now include _____

_____

_____

_____

Things we didn't have then: Instead, we used:

    Computer   _____

    CD player   _____

    Photocopier   _____

    Touch-tone phone   _____

_____   _____

_____   _____

_____   _____

Some prices I remember are

Item   Price

_____ _____

_____ _____

_____ _____

_____ _____

_____ _____

Other things that have changed are _____

_____

_____

_____

_____

_____

_____

_____

_____

_____

_____

_____

_____

_____

_____

_____

LASTING THOUGHTS

Use the next four pages to write down thoughts that you would like to leave for your grandchildren. They could be words of advice and wisdom or thoughts on how to be successful in life. What would you like your grandchildren to remember most about you and your life? What are your wishes for them as they grow?

_____

_____

_____

_____

_____

_____

_____

_____

_____

_____

_____

_____

_____

_____

_____

It is not your obligation to complete the task of perfecting the world,
but neither are you free to desist from doing all you can.
(Pirke Avot [Ethics of the Fathers] 2:21)

לֹא עָלֶיךָ הַמְּלָאכָה לִגְמֹר וְלֹא אַתָּה בֶן חוֹרִין לְהִבָּטֵל מִמֶּנָה

PHOTOGRAPHS, MEMENTOS, and RECIPES

By virtue of three things does the world endure: truth, justice, and peace.
(Pirke Avot [Ethics of the Fathers] 1:17)

עַל שְׁלֹשָׁה דְבָרִים הָעוֹלָם קַיָּם: עַל הָאֱמֶת וְעַל הַדִּין וְעַל הַשָּׁלוֹם

Even if the kugel doesn't quite work out, you still have the noodles.
(Shalom Aleichem)

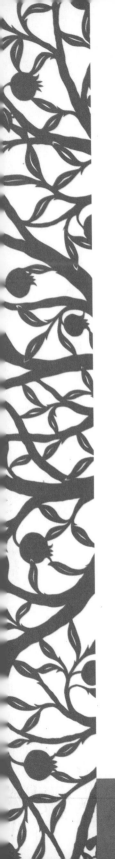

Look not at the flask but at what it contains. (Pirke Avot [Ethics of the Fathers] 4:27)

אַל תִּסְתַּכֵּל בַּקַּנְקַן אֶלָּא בַּמֶּה שֶׁיֶּשׁ בּוֹ